Journey

Elysia Dunford

BookLeaf Publishing

Presentation by *BookLeaf Publishing*

Web: www.bookleafpub.com

E-mail: info@bookleafpub.com

ISBN: 9789357211789

First edition 2023

DEDICATION

I dedicate this to you, to me, to we <3

ACKNOWLEDGEMENT

I'd like to acknowledge all we've faced, all we've overcome, the battles we have lost and those we have won, the people we have met, the faces we have seen, the places we have been, the things we have done, the things we wish we hadn't done, the wishes we have made, the wishes we have made come true, the good vibes we have sent and those we have received, the tears we have wept, the screams we have screamed, the hugs we have hugged, the kisses we have kissed, the yawns we have yawned, the sighs we have sighed, and how damn hard we have tried, the smiles we have smiled and seen, the laughter we have laughed and heard, the ah-choo's and the bless you's, all the pain we released and all that is still inside.

PREFACE

May we feel we are enough, may we feel joy
and expand our hearts, may we cruise around in
the infinite, may we let go, may we be free

May we experience magic and enjoy the mystery

Allure

She said you can drink the poison baby
Cuz I got the cure. I didn't even care if it was
just a lure
As soon as I tasted her lips I knew it was a lie,
But to stop drinking didn't even cross my mind
The more I drank, the thirstier I became
So I sped up my pace, there was only me to
blame
I couldn't drink fast enough so I started to inhale
My vision blurred so I read her like braille
The poison filled my lungs. I didn't try to run
From the moment I first saw her
I decided she had won

Ice Queen

Ice queen ice queen
Wishes she could melt
Sets fires to herself
A few drops trickle down
Then she straightens her crown
She's walking through hell
And still
She can't melt

Casual Love

You're tossing and turning in bed
I'm tossing and turning in my head
You steal the covers
I don't even care
It makes me smile as my hand brushes your hair

Casual that's what we are
But I don't sleep casually in your bed
Or daydream casually in my head
Wearing your sweater makes me feel all warm
and fuzzy
When we take selfies it makes me all buzzy

I can't casually put my arms around you or
casually bite my lip the way you like me to
I don't care if my smile is loud
And when you kissed me in that parking lot I
was damn proud

And I wonder if you can tell
I don't know how to casually love you

Surrender

Every challenge is an opportunity.
Have faith in God, the universe, source.
Let yourself be held tenderly with so much love.
Surrender to infinity

You

Every little bit of you is awe-some
There are no bad parts
Every little thing you feel is valid
You are made of love

You are so worthy
You are so loved
Take back your power
Radiate with love

Ah-choo!

I have an issue
I don’t have a tissue
My nose can’t be blown away

Mmmm

I'm like toxic waste
You can't just bury me and move on
I seep into your water and your plants
And poison you sweetly, slowly, gently

Mmmm

I taste like pie and I get you high so you'll keep
Breathing in the smoke screen of hope
Aw baby. I know I'm your favourite dope
But didn't your mama tell you drugs were bad
Even the best you've ever had

Figure 8

Our first kiss was in a closet
His little brother trapped us inside
But he has since come out of the closet
I didn't even know I was in there
And I'm still not too sure
But I mean
I liked her
And I liked it
So...I guess I'm...something
Not straight
Maybe a figure eight

Shark

She's a stalker, you better block her
She's a shark in the water, her mother's daughter
You better take heed not to bleed
Cuz once she's on to your scent, believe me she's hell-bent
Not a prayer in the world will save your doomed little heart from being violently ripped apart
So take note of what I've said
Because no one can help you when you're dead

I'm Hurting Me More

It's funny but it's not
I'm so scared of hurting him but I'm hurting me more
I'm hurting me more but I won't go
I'm hurting me more but oh no no
I'm hurting me more but I will stay
I'm hurting me more but I'll lead him on anyway
She says he's falling in love with you
I don't want to hear it cuz I know it's fucking true
So blindfold me, gag me, help me pretend that it's okay
It will all be over soon enough anyway

Gramma

My gramma in Tampa
Eats tahini in a bikini
And has a thing for teeny weenies
She snorts coke from her pinky
And bounces back like a slinky

Inside of me

You throw me up and I shove you down
All the way into the ground
You come right back
I toss you to the left and say go away
You pop up on my right and tell me that you're
here to stay
I run for the hills
But you're waiting at the top
So I roll to the bottom
But then when I stop
I look up
And what do I see?
You staring back at me
I run far and wide
But stop short of breath
As my heart beats out of my chest
My vision narrows
I can barely see
Yet still I feel you there
Inside of me

Magical Island

When your walls come crumbling down and
You let me into your inner world
The warmth reassures me that I am liked
And your spirit shines so bright
I bask in it and
Everything just feels so right
Not only right
But magical too
A special island, population: 2

Test Subject

Let me be
Your test subject
I'll let you test it all on me
Your hate, your love, your pain, your mercy
As long as it's yours

Validate

Validate me, validate me
I need you to not fucking hate me
Give me your stamp, now yours, and yours and yours and yours!
Ahhhh-pproved
What does that even prove?
Just that I can make you like me
But stamp me, stamp me
Until I'm drenched in ink and my skin won't hold anymore
Sopping wet, dripping on the floor
Just follow the trail of likeability
And there you'll find me
Poisoned and insecure
Endlessly searching for the cure

HAHAHA

Outside I'm laughing
Inside I'm hailing
And I feel like I'm constantly failing
Just keep swimming
Just keep swimming
In the shark infested waters
With bleeding wounds
You might be going further into the abyss
Swimming toward your demise
But you can't just stay put
No one can hear your cries

Cacophonic Symphony

Her disposition says that nothing's wrong
But in her head there's a different song
One with not enough rests and too many repeats
Dissonant chords and erratic beats
Some notes are too sharp, others too flat
The range is huge and the tempo too fast

The pain wells up in her eyes
As she lays here and writes
She's really not okay, she's really not fine
But she goes on like she is, like there's nothing to hide

The pain is familiar, a constant in her life
There is hate, horror, and distorted comfort in her strife
She is banged and bruised and internally scarred
But she keeps on driving that stupid fucking car

They see her smooth skin, not the wrinkles in her brain
They see her flowy hair, not the clots in her veins
They see the openness in her heart, not the tightness in her chest

They hear the lightness of her voice, not the heaviness of her breath
They see the brightness in her eyes, not the darkness when she cries
They don't see all the truths, but they don't see lies

Her touch may be tender but her grasp is tight
She wants to be loved and she loves to be right

It's easy to see the steps she takes forward, not the times she's regressed
Feel the love she gives, not all that's repressed
The hope and the joy, not the fear and the dread
Her clear advice, not the chaos in her head
The peace and quiet, not the chatter in her brain
That torments her and drives her insane

Life is but a Dream (*Sweetheart)

I said
I need a needle and a thread
So that I can sew it back together
Not broken, just fragmented
There's just holes in the whole
Splits at the seams
In the fabric of this dream

Underneath all the holes is a whole new layer
That can never be split
Because it's all that is
One is all
So all is one

Sunflower

Be like a sunflower
Turn toward the warmth and light
And watch as you grow to incredible heights

LGBT

A community
One that gives me confidence to be more me
Inspired, I aspire to be free
To unleash my truth, all parts of me

Walk with Pride

Walk with pride
Take things in stride
Laugh, laugh, laugh
Spread good vibes

www.ingramcontent.com/pod-product-compliance
Lightning Source LLC
Chambersburg PA
CBHW051758130826
49812CB00033B/1188
9789357211789